100 Cool Things about Bugs

By Shirley Siluk

First published in 2011 by freetothink books

freetothinkbooks.com

Gulf Breeze, FL 32563

For Noah

Table of Contents

1. Yum Yum

E ver look at a grasshopper or ant and think, **"Mmm, that looks delicious"**? Maybe you haven't, but plenty of other people around the world have. It's actually a smart food choice, considering that some bugs – when they're dead and dried up – can be more nutritious than meat or fish!

2. Did you know ...
Insects for dinner (or snacktime) are especially popular in parts of Africa and Asia. Top five choices on the **buggy menu**: Beetles, ants, bees, grasshoppers and crickets.

3. Do you like chocolate, apples, potatoes or pumpkin pie? Then be very happy we have insects called "pollinators." These kinds of bugs – including certain bees and flies – carry powdery pollen from the flower of one plant to another. **Without this exchange of pollen, some plants couldn't form seeds or fruits** ... which means we wouldn't have cacao (used to make chocolate), pumpkins, apples and many other popular fruits.

4. Did you know ...
Some people believe that if we **ate more insects** – and less beef, chicken, pork and fish – it would actually be better for both us and the planet. Not only are bugs leaner than other, more familiar types of meat, but they are easier to raise and cause less damage to the environment.

5. You might not have heard of the cochineal (COTCH-in-eel) bug, but chances are good you've eaten it! An insect that lives on cactus plants in Mexico and parts of South America, the cochineal has been used for a long

Fig. 1. Indio que recoge la Cochinilla con una colita de Venado. Fig 2. dicha. Fig. 3. Xicalpestle en que aparan la Cochinilla.

7

time to make a red coloring for food, fabrics and makeup. The next time you eat a snack food with a reddish color, read the ingredient label. If you see a name like "carmine," "cochineal extract," "natural red 4" or "crimson lake," that red color probably came from the **dried and ground-up bodies of cochineal bugs**.

6. Did you know ...
You need about **70,000 cochineal bugs** to make just one pound of dye for coloring? Cochineal dye comes in different shades of red, depending upon how the insects are killed, dried and treated.

7. Bumblebees can send messages to their fellow bumblebees by **smells they leave behind on flowers**. If a bee has taken lots of nectar from a flower, it can leave behind a scent that tells other bees, "Don't bother – no more food here!' " Bumblebees that find lots of good eating in one place, such as a tree full of nectar-rich blooms, can also mark a flower with a scent that says, "This is a great place to eat!"

8. Did you know ...
Bumblebees suck up nectar with their hair-tipped tongues, but the

only time you'll usually see a bee's tongue is when it's eating. The rest of the time, the tongue is folded up under the bumblebee's head and body. **Bee tongues come in all sorts of different sizes.** Bumblebees with long tongues can reach way down into flowers where the nectar is too deep for bees with shorter tongues.

9. Dung beetles **eat mostly poop** ("dung" is another word for poop). In fact, for some types of dung beetles, that's the only thing they eat. It might sound gross, but it's a good thing for people. By eating dung left on the ground by animals like cows or elephants, these beetles can prevent flies and other pests from hatching. And by burying poop underground for their babies to eat, dung beetles help make the soil healthier for farming.

10. Did you know ...
People in ancient Egypt often wore **dung beetle-shaped jewelry for good luck**. Egyptians back then thought that beetles rolling dung

resembled the god they believed rolled the sun across the sky every day. (Dung beetles roll poop into a ball, which they bury and lay their eggs in.)

2. Superbugs

What's the biggest bug ever? Around 390 million years ago – way before the dinosaurs – **giant sea scorpions more than 8 feet long** swam in the world's rivers and lakes. That's taller than the tallest man alive today! (Not actually a "bug," this super-size creepy-crawly was more closely related to today's scorpions and spiders, which are arachnids, not insects.)

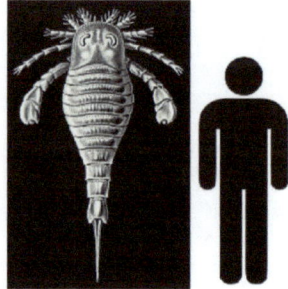

12. Did you know ...
Many other giant bugs lived around 300 million years ago: 3 ½-inch long cockroaches, dragonflies with wings 2 ½ feet across and **millipedes more than 6 feet long**. Scientists believe insects were able to grow so large because there was much more oxygen in the air back then.

13. Why aren't any insects today as big as they once were? Because bugs don't breathe air through a single trachea (air passage) into lungs like we do. They breathe in and out through holes called spiracles, which draw oxygen into tubes throughout their bodies. The bigger the insect, the bigger those tracheal tubes have to be to make sure every part of its body receives the oxygen it needs. At some point, if the bug were to become any larger, its body parts wouldn't have room for all

the air passages it needed. Back in the Paleozoic, though, there was **a whole lot more oxygen in the atmosphere** – 35 percent compared to the 21 percent we have today. That means insects' tracheal tubes didn't need to be as big as they are today to make sure bugs got enough oxygen. Easier oxygen = bigger bugs!

14. While ants can lift many times their own weight, one kind of dung beetle is even stronger. How mighty is this musclebound bug? It can pull an object that weighs 1,141 times more than it does. That would

be **like your mom pulling six school buses at once** across your school's parking lot!

15. Did you know ...
Even these super-bugs can't stay super-strong if they don't eat right. After a couple of days on a poor diet, **strong beetles turn into weaklings**.

16. Know why cockroaches are so hard to smoosh? Because they're awfully fast for their size. One American cockroach was clocked at a top speed of 3.4 miles per hour. That might not sound fast, but for a critter just 1½ inches long, that's around 50 times its body length every second. A person going that fast would be **a superhero who could run 210 miles per hour!**

17. Did you know ...
There are more than **4,500 different kinds of cockroaches** in the world. One of the largest is the Madagascar hissing cockroach, which can grow up to four inches long and can live for up to five years. Because these kinds of cockroaches don't bite, can't fly and make cool hissing noises, some people like to keep them as pets.

18. What's the loudest insect you're ever likely to meet? An African species of cicada called Brevisana brevis holds the record, with a call that reaches 106.7 decibels when heard from a distance of 50 centimeters (just under 20 inches). That's **louder than a jackhammer**, and getting close to the point where sound could actually cause your ears to hurt.

19. Can you believe a tropical bug holds the record for the insect best able to survive the cold? An African fly known as the sleeping chironomid starts its life in shallow ponds that often dry up. As a result, the larvae (babies) can stay dried up for a long time – up to 17 years – and still live. Dried larvae can even be **dunked in liquid helium** – which has a super-cold temperature of 270 degrees below zero Celsius (that's 454 degrees below zero in Fahrenheit!) – for up to five minutes and later bounce back to life.

20. Did you know ...

Sleeping chironomid larvae can also survive heat of up to 102 degrees Celsius (more than 215 degrees Fahrenheit), radiation that hurts most other living things and **even a vacuum**, which means there's no air to breathe. Because of their amazing survival skills, these bugs are sometimes taken into space to be studied.

3. Take a Number

There are almost 7 billion people living on Earth in 2012, but care to guess how many insects are on the planet? Famous scientist E. O. Wilson thinks our world might be home to **10,000,000,000,000,000,000 (that's 10 quintillion!)** in all. That's way more than one billion insects for every human! Scientists have identified more than one million different kinds of insects, but they believe there might be many more we haven't found yet ... maybe as many as 30 million more different types.

22. Did you know ...
That even though we usually use the words "bug" and "insect" to mean the same thing, they're not! True bugs – which belong to an order of insects called Heteroptera – are **just a small part of the bigger insect family**.

23. No other insect on the planet comes together in bigger crowds – known as "swarms" in the bug world – than the desert locust. In 1954, Africa saw the largest swarm ever measured: **10 billion locusts** covering an area of 200 square kilometers (almost as big as 45,000 football playing fields put together). That's nearly 223,000 bugs per football field!

24. Did you know ...
The weird thing about the swarming desert locust is that it normally lives alone, not in huge groups. When the right amount of rain causes the right amount of plants to grow, though, the locust changes: young insects change from green to yellow-and-black, and the grownups change from brown to red or yellow. Along with the change in color,

13

the locusts also start giving off a scent that attracts them to one another. This causes them to suddenly come together in huge swarms that can **eat up almost every kind of plant and crop in their paths.**

Solitary

Gregarious

25. How much would all the world's insects weigh if we could gather them up and put them on a gigantic scale? Canadian entomologist Brian Hocking once estimated they might add up to **2.7 billion tons** – way more than the weight of all of the world's people!

26. Did you know ...
By weight, ants alone account for 15 to 20 percent of all the animal life on Earth. In tropical areas, they can make up **more than 25 percent of all the area's biomass**, which is a word for how much all living things put together weigh.

27. The bed bug is a kind of insect that likes eating human blood. It's a pest whose bite can be irritating to humans, but it isn't known to carry any dangerous diseases. What's strange about bed bugs is that they stopped being a problem in places like the US and Europe more than 50 years ago. Lately, though, they've **started making a comeback**. Scientists believe that's probably because people are traveling more, and the bed bugs they encounter in different parts of the world are becoming more resistant to insecticides that once controlled these pests.

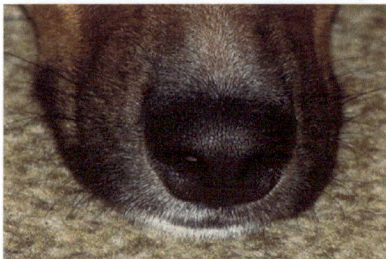

28. Did you know ...
Some people say an infestation of bed bugs **smells like almonds, overripe raspberries or something that's obnoxiously sweet**. That's a good thing, because trained dogs (which have such a keen sense of smell) can

often identify a bed bug problem far faster than human inspectors can, thanks to the insects' unique smell.

29. There are close to **3,000 different kinds of termites in the world**, and all of them eat some form of tough plant fiber, called cellulose. While they can cause lots of damage to buildings and other wooden structures, they can also do good. Termites in Africa, for example, eat so many of the leaves and wood litter that fall to the ground that they actually help reduce the threat of bush fires.

30. Did you know ...
Scientists think **termites could help us find new ways to make fuel**. Thanks to the bacteria that live in their digestive systems, termites can digest tough materials like wood and paper ... and produce hydrogen gas as waste. Hydrogen is a clean-burning fuel that can be used to power cars and other specially designed vehicles, without generating the pollution that today's gasoline-driven cars do.

4. Ancient and Amazing

You know how you can leave an impression of your hand by pressing it down into wet sand or mud? Well, an insect that lived more than 300 million years ago did something kind of like that when it landed on a muddy surface. The print it left behind in that mud, which later turned into stone, is the **oldest impression of a flying bug** that scientists have ever found.

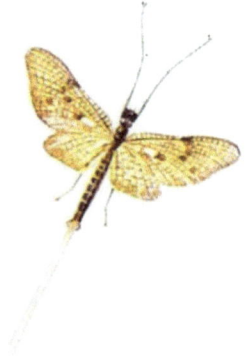

32. Did you know ...
Fossils of insects and other creatures can turn up in the strangest places, because parts of the world that are icy cold or mountainous today **could have been tropical forests and ocean shorelines millions of years ago**. That 300-million-year-old bug impression? Scientists found it in a field behind a shopping mall in Massachusetts.

33. How much heat can some insects take? Not many can beat the Sahara Desert ant, which can remain active with **a body temperature of more than 50 degrees C** (that's 122 degrees F!). That comes in handy, considering the desert surface where it lives can reach up to 70 degrees C (a whopping 158 degrees F) at the hottest point of the day.

34. Did you know ...
Scientists believe Sahara Desert ants have managed to push heat tolerance **about as far as possible for most animals on our planet**. Only single-celled or microscopic creatures known as thermophiles (from the Greek words for "heat" and "love") can beat them; these tiny heat-lovers thrive at temperatures of up to 80 degrees C (176 degrees F)!

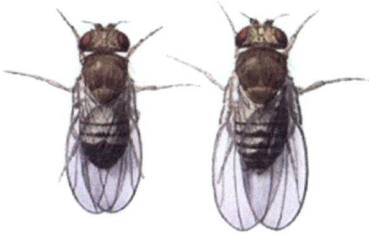

35. Few animal species on Earth have been studied more than the fruit fly, and it's not because scientists especially enjoy working with tiny, red-eyed insects. Fruit flies are small, cheap and easy to raise, which helps keep research costs low. They take **only about 10 days to go from egg to egg-laying adult**, which means less time needed to track changes from generation to generation (that is, from parent to child to grandchild to greatgrandchild and so on). And females can lay a lot of eggs in a short time period – as many as 100 per day – which makes population experiments a lot easier to conduct.

36. Did you know ...
That the fruit fly beats the cockroach hands down (or is it six legs down?) when it comes to surviving a nuclear disaster? While cockroaches have long enjoyed the reputation of being able to survive anything, even an atomic bomb explosion, they're not as tough or radiation-resistant as the common fruit fly. In fact, studies have found that fruit flies can probably survive **10 times as much radiation as cockroaches**.

37. How many cartoons have you seen where a character escapes a swarm of angry bees by diving into the nearest pond until the insects give up and fly away? In real life, it turns out, getting away from bees on the attack isn't that easy. Africanized honey bees – **so-called "killer bees"** – for example, will simply wait around until you come up for air, then go on the attack again. It's better to protect your face and run to a shelter of some kind as quickly as possible.

38. Did you know ...
That fire ants are another kind of insect that won't let water stop them. When it looks like their colony is threatened by flooding, these types of ants will quickly come together, hanging onto one another using their

claws, sticky leg pads and pinching jaws ("mandibles"), to form a floating, living mat that can safely drift to a new and drier location. These ant rafts don't sink because the rough, hairy texture of the ants' bodies helps trap air and keeps them floating. Scientists believe these floating getaway mats could include **hundreds of thousands of ants**.

39. Like its name suggests, the bombardier beetle is good at shooting its enemies. Its weapon of choice is a combination of two chemicals it keeps in separate chambers near its rear end. When the beetle feels threatened, it squeezes muscles to mix those two chemicals, with explosive results: a liquid-gas blend that **smells bad and heats up to near-boiling temperatures**. The bug can fire that mix in almost any direction, and you can actually hear a popping noise when it "shoots." The hot, stinky and irritating mixture can kill some insects and can be painful for humans who are caught in the crossfire.

40. Did you know ...
The bombardier beetle can **hit a target from almost any direction**. It also doesn't seem to be at all bothered by the irritating chemicals it shoots at others. Scientists still aren't sure why.

5. Cuddly They're Not

What kind of animals make the best pets? You might say "dog" or "cat," but in other parts of the world, people think of crickets, praying mantises and stick insects. Crickets have been especially popular pets in places like Japan and China. Why? **They're easy to take care of, don't need much space and make music.** (Crickets – only the boys – "sing" by rubbing their wings together.)

42. Did you know ...
Pet crickets also **make good burglar alarms**. Because they stop chirping when a noise disturbs them, crickets can let their owners know when someone is trying to break into the house.

43. Scientists who study bugs can help police detectives solve crimes. Called **"forensic entomologists,"** these scientists look for fly eggs, maggots and other insects on dead bodies. Depending on how many bugs – and what types – they find, these specialists can figure out how long a person or animal has been dead.

44. Did you know ...
Bugs found at an accident or crime scene can also **provide evidence of things like explosives**. By testing the insects' bodies in a laboratory, scientists can detect signs of many different chemicals.

45. After flies lay their eggs, the eggs quickly hatch into maggots – small, worm-like creatures that will eventually grow up into flies themselves. Maggots **have a taste for dead flesh**, but that's not necessarily a bad thing: doctors sometimes use them to clean out

19

wounds that won't heal. While it sounds disgusting, it does the trick. Called maggot therapy, this kind of treatment gets rid of dead skin and leaves behind only living flesh that has a much better chance of healing.

46. Did you know ...
It once was a tradition among some people in Mexico to **dress fleas in tiny clothes**. You won't find many people who practice

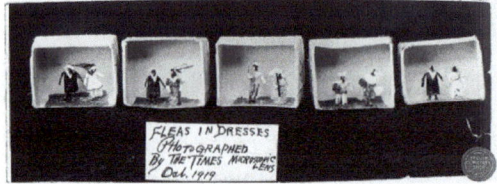

this art, called pulgas vestidas, anymore, but you can still see photographs of these tiny, dressed-up insects in some art exhibits and museums.

47. Beetles in nature come in a wide variety of colors, but some cultures have decided to improve on that by turning them into **living jewelry**. In Mexico, for example, some people stick rhinestones – or even real precious gems and gold – onto the backs of beetles, then attach a little chain to the bug so it can be worn as "jewelry" without the decoration walking or flying away.

48. Did you know ...
While it might sound cool, **bringing a jeweled bug across the border is against the law**. (Not to mention that bugs are probably be happier without chains and heavy decorations.) That's because countries want to avoid "invasive species" – creatures that don't naturally live there.

These kinds of species can cause all sorts of trouble for local wildlife and can sometimes even help kill them off.

49. What are some of the world's ugliest bugs? A couple of annual contests – one in Flagstaff, Arizona, the other in Oklahoma – have named these the **tops in ugly**: snakefly, tick, wheelbug, robber fly, mole cricket, weevil, cottonwood borer, velvet ant and jerusalem cricket.

50. The only thing an adult flea eats is **blood**.

6. Creepy, Weird and Spooky

There are parts of the Amazon Rainforest in South America where you'll find only one type of plant, and no other ... and it's all because of ants. Lemon ants create these special forest areas – called **devil's gardens** – by injecting a poison into the leaves of all the other kinds of plants. The poison, called formic acid, starts killing the plants within one day. Why do these ants do that? Because the trees they don't kill have hollow stems that make perfect nests for ant colonies. The largest devil's garden scientists have found so far has more than 300 trees in it and is around 800 years old.

52. Did you know ...
Devil's gardens got that name because some people who live in the Amazon believe those places are home to **an evil spirit that can trick people into getting lost**. (By the way, the ants that make those gardens are called lemon ants because that's kind of what they taste like: lemons.)

53. The **deathwatch beetle** has a spooky-sounding name, but that's not the reason people should be worried about seeing the bug in their house. This tiny bug – usually no longer than 3/8 of an inch in length – lays its eggs in wood, and the larvae that hatch can tunnel through the wood, eating it as they go. Over time, these small creatures can cause serious damage to homes and furniture.

54. Did you know ...
That the deathwatch beetle apparently got its ominous name from the tapping sound it makes (by hammering its head against wood) to attract a mate. Long ago, deathwatch beetles could be heard tapping in old buildings on quiet nights, when people might be sitting by the bedside of someone who was very sick. When family members heard that tapping sound, they thought it was **an omen that the sick person might die**.

55. Female fleas need to mate only once, and can then keep laying eggs – up to 50 a day – for the rest of their lives. There are **more than 2,000 different kinds of fleas** in the world. While we tend to think of dogs suffering from fleas the most, the most common form of flea found in the US is actually the cat flea.

56. Assassin bugs can be as deadly as their name suggests. They eat other insects – even much larger ones – by capturing them and injecting them with **poisonous saliva**, which turns the prey's insides into a sort-of soup. After that, the assassin sucks out the "soup" for dinner.

57. A few kinds of assassin bugs prefer to **drink blood from animals or people**. Some of these, called "kissing bugs," tend to bite sleeping people on the lips.

58. Did you know ...
Some assassin bugs attack their prey by pretending to be ... dinner. One kind climbs onto a spider web and wiggles the sticky threads to make the spider think it's trapped. When the spider creeps closer to try and grab a meal, the assassin bug grabs and bites it so it can suck up **a serving of spider soup**.

59. Brain-eating human zombies make for great spooky stories, but being "zombified" is a real threat for some insects. One kind of

fungus, for example, has been **"zombifying" ants for at least 48 million years**. The fungus forces infected ants to march down from their nests high in jungle trees to leaves just above the ground. The infection then makes the ants bite down on a low-hanging leaf, where they continue to hang after they die. After a few weeks of growing inside a dead ant's body, a stroma – a clump of fungus seeds – sprouts through its shell, ready to infect the next generation of zombie ants.

60. Did you know ...
That one kind of fly can turn ants into even more gruesome zombies? The tiny phorid fly looks for an ant victim and swoops down to lay a single egg in the ant's head. The developing larva takes control of the ant's body, first forcing it to walk far away from the rest of the ant colony. As the larva grows and eats the ant's brain from the inside, the ant dies. Eventually, **the ant's head falls off** and the next generation zombie-creating fly emerges to repeat the cycle.

7. Deceiving Appearances

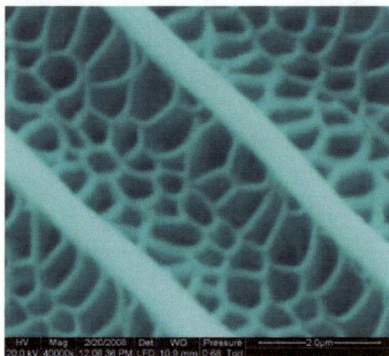

Butterfly wings might look colorful, but appearances can fool you. The brilliant hues in many butterfly wings aren't real colors, but tricks of light. The scales on some butterfly wings are often brown or black ... but they **reflect light like a crystal**, making the wings look blue or green or red.

62. Did you know ...
Scientists have actually used the trick of butterfly wings to **make better solar panels**. By imitating how wing scales reflect light, we can create solar cells that capture more power from the sun to make electricity.

63. A Madagascar hissing cockroach hisses by **pushing air hard its breathing pores**. Most other insects that make noise do so by vibrating body parts or rubbing parts together.

64. Did you know ...
Not all the bugs we call flies are "true flies." That name is used only for the ones with two wings. Other bugs that aren't true flies have four wings: two in the front, two in the back (like butterflies have). You can also tell who's who by a bug's common name. **True flies have two-word names** – fruit fly, house fly, crane fly, etc. – while other "flies" have one-word names like butterfly, dragonfly and stonefly.

65. You've probably never heard a butterfly, but some of these beautiful insects actually do make noise. One type of butterfly in Venezuela, for example, makes clicking sounds to help it recognize other butterflies of the same kind around it. And **the peacock**

butterfly can make a hissing noise by rubbing parts of its wings together, much like crickets do.

66. Did you know ...
If some butterflies make sounds, **that must mean they can hear too**. The clicking butterflies, for instance, have a body part under their wings that acts kind of like our eardrums. And certain butterflies that fly at night can hear very high-pitched noises that we can't. They use that ability to avoid bats, which also come out at night, have excellent hearing and like to eat insects.

67. What's the world's most deadly bug? Believe it or not, it's not some rare poisonous wasp or killer bee, but the ordinary mosquito. There are more than 3,000 different kinds of mosquitoes in the world, and a small number of these help to spread deadly human diseases. Just one kind of mosquito – the Anopheles – carries malaria from person to person, causing fever in **about 250 million people a year**.

68. Did you know ...
That mosquitoes usually live by eating just nectar? To be able to lay eggs and have babies, though, certain types of female mosquitoes also need to **drink blood from animals**. So the next time you discover an itchy mosquito bite on your arm or leg, remember it's because there's a Mama Mosquito out there somewhere who's hoping to lay eggs.

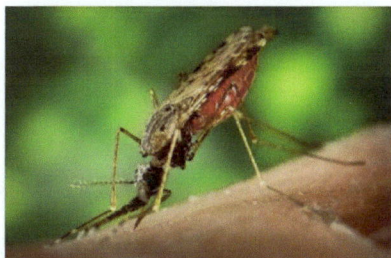

69. What's not to like about ladybugs? They're pretty, don't bite and are considered great helpers for home-gardeners who want to get rid of plant-eating aphids. Ladybugs, though, aren't complete ladies, it turns out. When they think an insect or another animal (even a human) is threatening them, they defend themselves in a nasty kind of way: **squeezing blood out of their bodies to freak out their enemie**s. Not just any blood, either, but a strangely colored (kind of orange and

yellow), stinky blood that can leave a stain on your clothes and belongings.

70. Did you know ...
Ladybugs, known in some places as ladybirds, can also create trouble for grape-growers who make wine. Wine is made by first crushing grapes ... and all that crushing inevitably squashes a few bugs along with the fruit. Ladybugs caught in a grape harvest release defensive chemicals when they're about to be smooshed, and that can make the wine taste really awful. Just a teeny, tiny bit can make a wine **smell or taste like cat pee** or peanut butter that's gone bad.

8. Strange Life

There's a reason mayflies were assigned to the scientific order Ephemeroptera, which comes from a Greek word (ephemeros) that means "short-lived" ... some types of these bugs have **an adult life only minutes long**. While they can live as babies (nymphs, they're called) for one to four years, mayflies don't have much of a life after they shed their nymph skins for the last time. One species, Dolania americana, has only about five minutes to spread its adult wings, find a mate and – if it's female – lay its eggs before it dies.

72. Did you know ...
With such a short adult lifespan, mayflies don't have time to build up an appetite, so they don't eat. In fact, some types **don't even have mouthparts.**

73. Scale insects have an even stranger life cycle. When the females of some species grow up, they lose their legs and turn into what some have called a tiny insect **"Jabba the Hutt."** It's even worse for the boys, though: the even tinier males die right after they mate with the females so they can lay eggs.

74. Do you like to read? Then you've probably been called a "bookworm" at some point. **There really are creatures known as bookworms**, though, and they're not at all kind to books. In fact, they can damage books, furniture and anything else made with paper or wood. Bookworms are actually not worms but insects (or insect larvae, which can look like worms), and they can be a pest in libraries, museums and other places. Some of these bugs, like the book louse, can be very tiny – as small as 1 millimeter in length. They don't actually eat the paper in books, but chew up the glue in the binding. (Oddly, though, book lice are more common in pantries, where they eat things like flour, than on bookshelves.)

75. Did you know ...
Many types of female book lice can lay eggs without having to mate. In fact, in at least one species (Liposcelis bostrychophilis), **all the adults are females** – not a single male in sight.

76. Pound for pound or, rather, ounce for ounce, bugs are more dependent on their eyes than almost any other creature on the planet. In some insects, eyes and eye-related parts account for almost one-third of body mass. That would be like a 100-pound person having **eyes weighing about 30 pounds**!

77. Did you know ...
That understanding how bug brains process information from their eyes could help us develop all kinds of cool new technology. For example, some scientists believe insects with fast visual responses could help us figure out how to **build cars that could "watch" the road** and automatically adjust the controls to avoid accidents.

78. Grownup bugs have some pretty good ways of getting away from trouble: some can run fast, many can fly and others sting or spray nasty poisons at their enemies. But what about insects who aren't grown up yet? Well, wormlike tiger beetle babies have found a great way to escape a would-be predator: **make like a wheel and roll**. By quickly coiling, uncoiling and then rolling into a loop again, a larva can hop away from anything that's bothering it, catch the wind and then ride the breeze to roll far away. On especially windy days, young tiger beetles can get such good momentum going that a person running after them can't keep up.

79. Did you know ...
That grown-up tiger beetles are super-speedy. In fact, tiger beetles have been clocked at **a top speed of 125 body lengths per second** ... which is, inch for inch, way faster than an Olympic star like Michael Johnson. While Johnson was able to reach a speed of 5.6 body lengths

per second, one type of tiger beetle from Australia can reach up to 125 body lengths per second. That's crazy fast.

80. Some flowering plants need certain insects as much as the insects need them. In fact, evidence from millions of years ago show that some bugs and flowering plants coevolved ... meaning they gradually developed a strong dependence on one another. The yucca plant, for example, **can be pollinated by only the yucca moth**, which eats only yucca seeds.

9. Tastes like Chicken

Like almonds? Then you might enjoy the flavor of cooked witchetty grubs (though other people say they taste a bit like scrambled eggs). An important part of the traditional Aboriginal Australian diet, witchetty grubs **can also be eaten raw**.

82. If the idea of chewing a **"salty, fruity, flowery Jolly Rancher"** appeals to you, then try biting into a giant water bug. That's how Dave Gracer, advisor for the website Insects are Food, describes their flavor.

83. Are you **a fan of fried pork rinds**? Then beetle larvae might be your favorite buggy treat. (Hint: if you're looking for some added fish flavor, look for beetle larvae that live in or around water.)

84. Yes, some bugs **do taste like chicken**. According to the authors of "Creepy Crawly Cuisine," certain butterfly and moth caterpillars can have a poultry flavor, though others are fishier in taste.

85. Maybe it's the crunch, but insects are often described as tasting like nuts of one kind or another. Ants, write the authors of "Creepy Crawly Cuisine," are **"almost always nutty."**

86. Mmm, lemony! A variety of Australian ant with a green abdomen tastes like lemons, or even – according to one taster – **lemon sherbet**.

87. If you don't mind the taste of soft-shell crabs (crabs that have just shed their old, hard shell and are cooked and eaten, new shell and all), you might enjoy **deep-fried Cambodian tarantula**, which supposedly has a similar flavor. (Tarantulas, like all spiders, are not in fact insects, but arachnids.)

88. Who doesn't like potato chips? If you're a fan of crunchy, salty treats, you'll probably also enjoy most types of **fried insects**, which bug-lovers say can be just as addictive for munching.

89. Like the idea of tasting rancid oil that **also leaves your mouth feeling numb** like you've just had a shot at the dentist's? Probably not ... so avoid chowing down on stinkbugs (like you'd want to anyway, with a name like that).

90. People don't eat bugs only when there's nothing much else to eat. In fact, many insect gourmets have favorites they say are downright tasty. According to those who know (that is, people who actually eat bugs on a regular basis), some of the yummiest species include the wax worm (wax moth larvae), which are so high in fat they're actually fattening; fried or roasted giant water beetles (they taste like scallops, some say); and toasted tayno kuro worms that, prepared the way they are in the Andes, reportedly **taste like charred hot dogs**.

10. Nice Times Six (Legs)

When you think about good animal moms, you don't usually think about insects. But the earwig is different from most bugs: after laying her eggs, an earwig mom will protect her young from predators, work constantly to keep her eggs clean and even **feed them with food from her own mouth** after they hatch. And if she happens to die before her babies are ready to strike out on their own, she herself will become a meal for her young.

92. The honeybee has been called the **"world's most beneficial insect,"** and it's no surprise why. Besides helping to pollinate a large number of crops, including most fruit trees, these bugs also produce the amazing product honey. Honey can be stored for many years and is being studied for its ability to fight some kinds of infections.

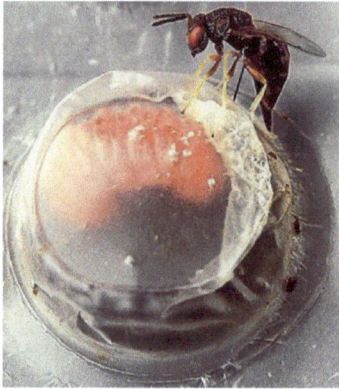

93. The name – parasitic wasp – doesn't sound very pleasant, but some of these insects can be a gardener's best friend. They kill and eat a lot of crop pests. In some cases, they even respond to **"cries for help"** from a plant under attack: when caterpillars start chewing on certain kinds of plants, their saliva mixes with the plant's juices to send an "alarm" scent that attracts parasitic wasps. A wasp catching the scent will fly to the plant, kill the caterpillar and sometimes even lay eggs in caterpillar's body.

94. Mantises, commonly called praying mantises because of how they hold up their large forearms, are another great predator of insect pests. They're not fussy eaters, either: big mantises have also been **known to eat lizards, frogs, birds and rodents**, among other things.

In Australia, geckos reportedly prefer to keep a safe distance from the native Australian mantis.

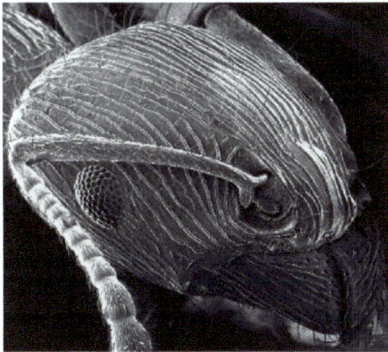

95. Some ants' powerful jaws, or "mandibles," have been used by people in India, South America and Africa to **stitch together wounds**. An ant would be held up to the injury that needed to be closed and allowed to clamp shut its jaws. The ant's body would then be pulled off, leaving the head and jaws on to keep the wound "stitched" together.

96. Dung beetles have helped reduce problems with flies in parts of Australia. Scientists first introduced the beetles to the country in the 1960s because cattle farming was creating **out-of-control amounts of cow poop**, which no local insects were interested in eating. By chowing down on all the excess poop, the dung beetles keep pastures cleaner and healthier for cows. The bugs also control the spread of nuisance bush flies by getting rid of fresh cow dung the flies like to lay their eggs in.

97. People who design robots get a lot of ideas by studying how insects move. Six-legged robots can move around in places where wheels won't work, and can keep going **even if one or two legs are damaged or destroyed**. Plus, because insects have much simpler nervous systems than other types of creatures, their behavior is easier to copy in robot form.

98. Where does silk – that sleek, shiny fabric – come from? Thank the domesticated silkmoth, whose babies (caterpillars known as "silkworms") create cocoons of thin, silky fiber that is used to make the material. People in Asia have been raising silkworms for thousands of years. In fact, the type of silkworm bred for making silk has become **totally dependent on people to survive**: they wouldn't last in the

wild because the grownup moths can't fly and they aren't naturally afraid of predators.

99. Bee stings are painful, but **bee venom might end up being good for us**. Researchers are studying if the poison from bees could help reduce pain and swelling in people who have arthritis and other ailments.

100. Mound-building termites use a clever design of inside chambers to control air flow and temperature in their mounds. Architects have found they can use the same idea to design buildings that stay at comfortable indoor temperatures without having to use a lot of energy for air-conditioning or heating. So **copying termites could help save energy** by making our buildings much more efficient.

Bonus Chapter: The Best Websites About Bugs

American Mosquito Control Association (http://www. mosquito.org/): The association's website tells you a lot more than how to get rid of these pests. It also offers information on mosquito types and biology, fun facts, bugs commonly mistaken for mosquitoes and a large number of links.

AntWeb (http://www.antweb.org/): In addition to an online catalog of the world's ants, this site from the California Academy of Sciences also features photos, educational resources and a really cool, interactive Google Earth plugin.

Ask a Biologist (http://askabiologist.asu.edu/): You can learn about more than just bugs here, but this site from Arizona State University offers plenty of interesting information, images and student research tools.

BugGuide.net (http://bugguide.net): A wealth of information, photographs and identification help about insects, arachnids and related creatures found across the US and Canada.

BugInfo.com (http://buginfo.com/): Focused mostly on household bugs from a pest control perspective, this site offers a wide variety of interesting articles about common insects.

Buglife (http://www.buglife.org.uk): A project of the Invertebrate Conservation Trust, Buglife is committed to raising awareness and promoting conservation of Britain's rare and "fascinating little animals."

Bugs for Dinner! (http://bugsfordinner.blogspot.com/): While it's no longer active, this blog features a lot of posts, complete with photos, about insects as food.

Bumblebee.org (http://bumblebee.org/): Extensive information about bumblebee species, habits, lifecycles, physical structure, endangered status and much more.

Encylopedia of Life (http://www.eol.org/pages/344): Being developed through an "an unprecedented global partnership" between scientists and the public, the Encyclopedia of Life aims to catalog every known species in the world. The encyclopedia's entry on insects leads to a wealth of information, photographs, videos, maps and more about bugs.

Entomological Society of America (http://www.entsoc.org/): The organization for professional entomologists (bug scientists) has a website with resources for teachers and the public, links and information for anyone considering studying insects as a career.

The Flea Circus Research Library (http://fleacircus.co.uk/): More information than you can ever imagine about flea circuses: history, fiction, films, games and more.

Insects Are Food (http://insectsarefood.com/): News, guides to edible bugs and – for the brave – recipes. As the site says, "Entomophagy is the future."

Insects As Food (http://www.food-insects.com): No longer being updated, this site provides information about food insects and related books, sites and other resources.

Insects.org (http://www.insects.org/): Lots of articles, photos, links and resources about insects.

Oklahoma Ugly Bug Home Page (http://www.uglybug.org/): Looking for microscopic closeups of insect heads and awards for which are the "ugliest"? This is the place.

PestWorldForKids.org (http://www.pestworldforkids.org): A child-oriented site with a glossary, photos, study guides, bug-related science-fair kits, resources for teachers and more.

Pollinator Partnership (http://pollinator.org/): A highly informative site for anyone interested in learning about – and protecting – pollinating species, insect and otherwise.

Purdue University's Annual Bug Bowl (http://extension.entm. purdue.edu/bugbowl/): Information about the university entomology department's annual Bug Bowl, the "largest known insect event of its kind."

Tree of Life Project (http://tolweb.org/Arthropoda/2469): The "Arthropoda" page lets you explore all the different scientific groups and subgroups of animals that we call "bugs." Extensive scientific references and links.

University of Florida Book of Insect Records (http://entnemdept.ufl.edu/walker/ufbir/index.shtml): A work in progress, this online resource offers an amazing variety of insect-related records, complete with scientific references and links.

Weird Foods from Around the World (http://www.weirdfood.com/ weird-food-bugs.html): The Weird Foods: Bugs pages features a nice summary of bug dishes eaten around the world, along with a few recipes.

What's That Bug? Insect Identification (http://whatsthatbug.com): A great place for learning more about the insects you encounter.

Wikipedia (http://en.wikipedia.org/wiki/Insect): The Wikipedia "Insect" entry is your best starting-off point for exploring everything there is to know about the insect world.

Index

Index

100 Cool Things about Bugs

Other freetothink book titles:

Prove It! Fact-Checking Secrets of a Fanatical Online Researcher (2014)

100 Cool Things About Zombies (2013)

100 Ways to Make Money Online: A Guide to the 'Net's Top Freelance Marketplaces, Crowdsourcing Work Sites and Places to Sell Your Stuff (2012)

Rhythms of Shadow and Light in a Time of Divorce, Occupy and Climate Change (2012)

For more information, visit freetothinkbooks.com

www.ingramcontent.com/pod-product-compliance
Lightning Source LLC
Chambersburg PA
CBHW041802040426
42448CB00001B/19